NEW YORK, NEW YORK

NEW YORK, NEW YORK
The City in Art and Literature

THE METROPOLITAN MUSEUM OF ART

UNIVERSE

The works of art reproduced in this book are from the collections of The Metropolitan Museum of Art unless otherwise noted.

FRONT COVER DETAIL, TITLE PAGE: *Flatiron in Summer*, 1948, printed 1975. Rudolf Burckhardt, American (b. Switzerland), 1914–1999. Gelatin silver print. The Elisha Whittelsey Collection, The Elisha Whittelsey Fund, 1975 1975.559.1. FRONT ENDPAPER: *Bird's-Eye View of the Great New York and Brooklyn Bridge, and Grand Display of Fireworks on Opening Night...*, 1883. A. Major, Publisher, American. Chromolithograph. The Edward W. C. Arnold Collection of New York Prints, Maps, and Pictures, Bequest of Edward W. C. Arnold, 1954 54.90.709. PAGE 5: *Metropolitan Museum, Central Park*, 1979. Richard Haas, American, b. 1936. Etching with aquatint. Gift of the artist, 1981 1981.1125. BACK ENDPAPER: *The Grand Display of Fireworks and Illuminations*, 1883. Currier and Ives, publishers, American. Chromolithograph. The Edward W. C. Arnold Collection of New York Prints, Maps, and Pictures, Bequest of Edward W. C. Arnold, 1954 54.90.779. BACK COVER: *Flatiron Building*, 1919. Samuel Halpert, American, 1884–1930. Oil on canvas. Gift of Dr. and Mrs. Wesley Halpert, 1981 1981.36.

First published in the United States of America by The Metropolitan Museum of Art, New York, and Universe Publishing, a division of Rizzoli International Publications, Inc., 300 Park Avenue South, New York, New York 10010.

First Edition
Printed in Hong Kong
09 08 07 06 05 04 03   5 4 3

Produced by the Department of Special Publications, The Metropolitan Museum of Art: Robie Rogge, Publishing Manager; William Lach, Editor; Anna Raff, Designer; Tatiana Ginsberg, Production Associate. All photography by The Metropolitan Museum of Art Photograph Studio unless otherwise noted.

Visit the Museum's Web site: www.metmuseum.org

Library of Congress Cataloging-in-Publication Data

New York, New York : the city in art and literature / edited by William Lach.
    p. cm.
    Includes illustrations of art works from the collections of the Metropolitan Museum of Art.
    ISBN 0-87099-966-4 (MMA) — ISBN 0-7893-0521-6 (Universe)
        1. American literature—New York (State)—New York. 2. City and town life—New York (State)—New York—Literary collections. 3. New York (N.Y.)—Literary collections. 4. New York (N.Y.)—Pictorial works. I. Lach, William, 1968- II. Metropolitan Museum of Art (New York, N.Y.)

PS509.N5 N5 2000
810.9'327471—dc21

00-055914

Contents

The Flatiron, 1904, printed 1909.
Edward Steichen, American
(b. Luxembourg), 1879–1973.
Gum bichromate over platinum print.
Alfred Stieglitz Collection, 1933 33.43.39

Foreword

This is an idiosyncratic ode to a place that continually asserts and redefines itself: New York, New York. Here, lithographs, photographs, paintings, and other works from The Metropolitan Museum of Art match writing about the city, including—in whole or in part—a letter to the editor and belles lettres; short stories and a multivolume history; poetry and the lyrics to a song or two.

More valentine than survey, this book is arranged alphabetically by author. Fortuitously, the collection opens with the historical Henry Adams and closes with the expansive Walt Whitman. For each match, the settings of the art and the writing are roughly the same, which gives a sharpened sense of both. By itself, Charles Dickens' question "Was there ever such a sunny street as this Broadway?" is a rhetorical device. Beside two contemporary prints of that thoroughfare, the question entices us to pick out pedestrians, trees, and building facades. Here, the street is what it was when Dickens wrote those words.

Something remains of this bright Broadway, but, beyond the obsolete omnibuses and cobblestones, something else—gentility?—has vanished. Wistfulness haunts even glimpses of Gotham not so far past: Toni Morrison's top-notch twenties New York, personified in James VanDerZee's Harlem ladies-who-lunch; Isaac Bashevis Singer's postwar Coney Island, beside Sid Grossman's shy, sly young couples on the sand; Oscar Hijuelos's 1950s mambo king, playing off of Garry Winogrand's El Morocco dance floor. Even the urban desolation of Li-Young Lee's 1990 love poem, highlighted in Per Bak Jensen's Fourteenth Street warehouses, seems almost quaint.

The one thing constant about New York is change, so ironically, nostalgia pervades all attempts to celebrate the place. Tourist or native, young or old, everyone who's been to this city has a New York story that defines this unstoppable, wonderful locality. This book is a stew of such tales, in art and in literature.

—*William Lach, Editor*

The New York Black Yankees, 1934. James VanDerZee, American, 1886–1983.
Gelatin silver print. Gift of James VanDerZee Institute, 1970   1970.539.58

Central Park, ca. 1908–10? Maurice Prendergast, American, 1858–1924.
Oil on canvas. George A. Hearn Fund, 1950 50.25

Introduction

In New York you can have anything you want, and even in the old days, you could, too, so that hasn't changed. You can also find anything that you're interested in here, and you don't have to have money to do so. But the thing I like best about New York is that you can meet all kinds of different people. I have all sorts of friends, and that's great fun.

When Vincent died, he left me the Foundation, and I had forty-five years with it. I decided that the money was made in New York, so I gave it away in New York. I loved doing it, because I went all over the city. I went down to SoHo, and I went up to Harlem, where some of the old ladies invite me to these extraordinary teas. People always came to me and talked about proposals, but I wanted to see how the Foundation's money was going to be used. And so I was up early in the morning, running around, never, never giving to something I didn't see. I've resigned from most everything now but the New York Public Library and the Metropolitan Museum. (I wanted to get off of the board of the Museum, because I thought I was getting too old, but they said no!) So here I am at ninety-eight, still running around.

I did things, not for the city so much, but for the people. I didn't go and build a building unless I knew the people and I knew what it was going to do for the people. And I gave—I don't know how much money, but quite a lot. I gave it all away; I haven't got any more left. Vincent said to me, "You're going to have a hell of a good time with it." And I did.

New York is a wonderful city.

—Interview with Brooke Astor, June 2000

At the end of a hundred leagues, we found a very pleasant site placed among some rising hills, in the midst of which there ran towards the sea a very large river, which was deep at its mouth, and from the sea to the hills there, on the flood tide, which we found eight feet, there might have passed ships of any burthen. . . . We proceeded with a boat to enter the river and land, which we found very populous, and the people much like the others, dressed with birds' feathers of diverse colors. They came towards us joyfully, emitting very great shouts of admiration, showing us where, with the boat, it was safest to land. . . . In a moment, as often happens in navigating, a violent contrary wind from the sea blowing up, we were forced to return to the ship, leaving the said land with much regret, considering that from its convenience and pleasant aspect it could not but have some valuable quality. . . .

—Giovanni da Verrazano
(translation J. C. Brevoort)

from History of the United States of America During the Administrations of Thomas Jefferson

If Washington Irving was right, Rip Van Winkle, who woke from his long slumber about the year 1800, saw little that was new to him, except the head of President Washington where that of King George had once hung, and strange faces instead of familiar ones. Except in numbers, the city was relatively no farther advanced than the country. Between 1790 and 1800 its population rose from 33,000 to 60,000; and if Boston resembled an old-fashioned English market-town, New York was like a foreign seaport, badly paved, undrained, and as foul as a town surrounded by the tides could be. Although the Manhattan Company was laying wooden pipes for a water supply, no sanitary regulations were enforced, and every few years—as in 1798 and 1803— yellow fever swept away crowds of victims, and drove the rest of the population, panic stricken, into the highlands. No day-police existed; constables were still officers of the courts; the night-police consisted of two captains, two deputies, and seventy-two men. The estimate for the city's expenses in 1800 amounted to $130,000. One marked advantage New York enjoyed over Boston, in the possession of a city government able to introduce reforms. Thus, although still mediaeval in regard to drainage and cleanliness, the town had taken advantage of recurring fires to rebuild some of the streets with brick sidewalks and curbstones. Travellers dwelt much on this improvement, which only New York and Philadelphia had yet adopted, and Europeans

Collect Pond, New York (detail), 1798. Archibald Robertson II, British, 1765–1835. Watercolor on off-white laid paper. The Edward W. C. Arnold Collection of New York Prints, Maps, and Pictures, Bequest of Edward W. C. Arnold, 1954 54.90.168. Photograph by Geoffrey Clements

agreed that both had the air of true cities: that while Boston was the Bristol of America, New York was the Liverpool, and Philadelphia the London. . . .

The city of New York was so small as to make extravagance difficult; the Battery was a fashionable walk, Broadway a country drive, and Wall Street an uptown residence. Great accumulations of wealth had hardly begun. The Patroon was still the richest man in the State. John Jacob Astor was a fur-merchant living where the Astor House afterward stood, and had not yet begun those purchases of real estate which secured his fortune. Cornelius Vanderbilt was a boy six years old, playing about his father's ferry-boat at Staten Island. New York city itself was what it had been for a hundred years past,—a local market.

—Henry Adams, American, 1838–1918

from **Becoming Intimate
with the Bohemians**

I stood on the corner of Sixth Avenue where it runs past Greenwich Avenue one night, and as I stood there a fur-trimmed woman, heavily laden with jewels, and two lanky daughters hailed me. In her eyes was a restlessness that was strange to me who have been used to looking into the quiet, often lazy, faces of those about me. Her eyes roved; so did the eyes of her daughters. There was a definite air of the loser looking for the lost.

"Where is Greenwich Village?" she asked, and she caught her breath.

"This is it," I answered, and I thought she was going to collapse.

"But," she stammered, "I have heard of old houses and odd women and men who sit on the curb quoting poetry to the policemen or angling for buns as they floated down into the Battery with the rain. I have heard of little inns where women smoke and men make love and there is dancing and laughter and not too much light. I have heard of houses striped as are the zebras with gold and with silver, and of gowns that——— Quick, quick!" she cried, suddenly breaking off in the middle of the sentence and grabbing a hand of either child exactly like the White Queen in *Through the Looking Glass* as she hurried forward. "There's one now!"

And so she left me in pursuit of a mere woman in a gingham gown with a portfolio under her arm.

—Djuna Barnes, American, 1892–1982

Seventh Avenue and Sixteenth Street, New York (detail), 1932. Mark Baum, American, 1903–2000.
Oil on canvas. Edith C. Blum Fund, 1983 1983.122.2

Invitation to Miss Marianne Moore

From Brooklyn, over the Brooklyn Bridge, on this fine morning,
    please come flying.
In a cloud of fiery pale chemicals,
    please come flying,
to the rapid rolling of thousands of small blue drums
descending out of the mackerel sky
over the glittering grandstand of harbor-water,
    please come flying.

Whistles, pennants and smoke are blowing. The ships
are signaling cordially with multitudes of flags
rising and falling like birds all over the harbor.
Enter: two rivers, gracefully bearing
countless little pellucid jellies
in cut-glass epergnes dragging with silver chains.
The flight is safe; the weather is all arranged.
The waves are running in verses this fine morning.
    Please come flying.

Come with the pointed toe of each black shoe
trailing a sapphire highlight,

Brooklyn Bridge, 1929, printed ca. 1970. Walker Evans, American, 1903–1975.
Gelatin silver print. Gift of Arnold H. Crane, 1972   1972.742.3

with a black capeful of butterfly wings and bon-mots,
with heaven knows how many angels all riding
on the broad black brim of your hat,
    please come flying.

Bearing a musical inaudible abacus,
a slight censorious frown, and blue ribbons,
    please come flying.
Facts and skyscrapers glint in the tide; Manhattan
is all awash with morals this fine morning,
    so please come flying.

Mounting the sky with natural heroism,
above the accidents, above the malignant movies,
the taxicabs and injustices at large,
while horns are resounding in your beautiful ears
that simultaneously listen to
a soft uninvented music, fit for the musk deer,
    please come flying.

For whom the grim museums will behave
like courteous male bower-birds,
for whom the agreeable lions lie in wait
on the steps of the Public Library,
eager to rise and follow through the doors
up into the reading rooms,
    please come flying.
We can sit down and weep; we can go shopping,
or play at a game of constantly being wrong
with a priceless set of vocabularies,
or we can bravely deplore, but please
    please come flying.

With dynasties of negative constructions
darkening and dying around you,
with grammar that suddenly turns and shines
like flocks of sandpipers flying,
     please come flying.

Come like a light in the white mackerel sky,
come like a daytime comet
with a long unnebulous train of words,
from Brooklyn, over the Brooklyn Bridge, on this fine morning,
     please come flying.

—Elizabeth Bishop, American, 1911–1979

The Brooklyn Bridge, 1910. Joseph Pennell, American, 1858–1926.
Lithograph. A. Hyatt Mayor Purchase Fund,
Marjorie Phelps Starr Bequest, 1981 1981.1030.2

Brooklyn Bridge, 1929, printed ca. 1970. Walker Evans, American, 1903–1975.
Gelatin silver print. Gift of Arnold H. Crane, 1972   1972.742.2

Washington Square, New York, 1938. André Kertész, American (b. Hungary), 1894–1985.
Gelatin silver print. Purchase, Rogers Fund, The Elisha Whittelsey Collection, The Elisha Whittelsey Fund, and
Mary Livingston Griggs and Mary Griggs Burke Foundation and Mrs. Vincent Astor Gifts, 1984 1984.1083.35

from Kafka Was the Rage

I think there's a great nostalgia for life in New York City, especially in Greenwich Village in the period just after World War II. We were all so grateful to be there—it was like a reward for having fought the war. There was a sense of coming back to life, a terrific energy and curiosity, even a feeling of destiny arising out of the war that had just ended. The Village, like New York City itself, had an immense, beckoning sweetness. It was like Paris in the twenties—with the difference that it was our city. We weren't strangers there, but familiars. The Village was charming, shabby, intimate, accessible, almost like a street fair. We lived in the bars and on the benches of Washington Square. We shared the adventure of trying to be, starting to be, writers or painters.

American life was changing and we rode those changes. The changes were social, sexual, exciting—all the more so because we were young. It was as if we were sharing a common youth with the country itself.

—Anatole Broyard, American, 1920–1990

from **Breakfast at Tiffany's**

Of course we'd never met. Though actually, on the stairs, in the street, we often came face-to-face; but she seemed not quite to see me. She was never without dark glasses, she was always well groomed, there was a consequential good taste in the plainness of her clothes, the blues and grays and lack of luster that made her, herself, shine so. One might have thought her a photographer's model, perhaps a young actress, except that it was obvious, judging from her hours, she hadn't time to be either.

Now and then I ran across her outside our neighborhood. Once a visiting relative took me to "21," and there, at a superior table, surrounded by four men, none of them Mr. Arbuck, yet all of them interchangeable with him, was Miss Golightly, idly, publicly combing her hair; and her expression, an unrealized yawn, put, by example, a dampener on the excitement I felt over dining at so swanky a place. Another night, deep in the summer, the heat of my room sent me out into the streets. I walked down Third Avenue to Fifty-first Street, where there was an antique store with an object in its window I admired: a palace of a bird cage, a mosque of minarets and bamboo rooms yearning to be filled with talkative parrots. But the price was three hundred and fifty dollars. On the way home I noticed a cab-driver crowd gathered in front of P. J. Clark's saloon, apparently attracted there by a happy group of whiskey-eyed Australian army officers baritoning, "Waltzing Matilda." As they sang they took turns spin-dancing a girl over the cobbles under the El; and the girl, Miss Golightly, to be sure, floated round in their arms light as a scarf.

—Truman Capote, American, 1924–1984

Models and Queensborough Bridge, New York, 1962, printed 1988. William Klein, American, b. 1928. Gelatin silver print. Gift of Arthur Stephen Penn and Marilyn Penn, 1991 1991.1343

The Green Car (detail), 1910. William Glackens, American, 1870–1938.
Oil on canvas. Arthur Hoppock Hearn Fund, 1937 37.73

from Coming, Eden Bower!

One bright December afternoon Eden Bower was going down Fifth Avenue in her car, on the way to her broker in William Street. Her thoughts were entirely upon stocks—Cerro de Pasco, and how much she should buy of it—when she suddenly looked up and realized that she was skirting Washington Square. She had not seen the place since she rolled out of it in an old-fashioned four-wheeler to seek her fortune, eighteen years ago.

"*Arrêtez, Alphonse. Attendez-moi,*" she called, and opened the door before he could reach it. The children who were streaking over the asphalt on roller skates saw a lady in a long fur coat and short, high-heeled shoes alight from a French car and pace slowly about the Square, holding her muff to her chin. This spot, at least, had changed very little, she reflected; the same trees, the same fountain, the white arch, and over yonder Garibaldi, drawing the sword for freedom. There, just opposite her, was the old red brick house.

"Yes, that is the place," she was thinking. "I can smell the carpets now, and that dog—what was his name? That grubby bathroom at the end of the hall, and that dreadful Hedger—Still, there was something about him, you know—"

She glanced up and blinked against the sun. From somewhere in the crowded quarter south of the Square a flock of pigeons rose, wheeling quickly upward into the brilliant blue sky. She threw back her head, pressed her muff closer to her chin, and watched them with a smile of amazement and delight. So they still rose, out of all that dirt and noise and squalor, fleet and silvery, just as they used to rise that summer when she was twenty and went up in a balloon on Coney Island!

Alphonse opened the door and tucked her robes about her. All the way down town her mind wandered from Cerro de Pasco, and she kept smiling and looking up at the sky.

—Willa Cather, American, 1873–1947

from **Opium's Varied Dreams**

There are 25,000 opium-smokers in the city of New York alone. At one time there were two great colonies, one in the Tenderloin, one of course in Chinatown. This was before the hammer of reform struck them. Now the two colonies are splintered into something less than 25,000 fragments. The smokers are disorganized, but they still exist.

The Tenderloin district of New York fell an early victim to opium. That part of the population which is known as the sporting class adopted the habit quickly. Cheap actors, race track touts, gamblers and the different kinds of confidence men took to it generally. Opium raised its yellow banner over the Tenderloin, attaining the dignity of a common vice.

Splendid "joints" were not uncommon then in New York. There was one on Forty-second street which would have been palatial if it were not for the bad taste of the decorations. An occasional man from Fifth avenue or Madison avenue would there have his private "layout," an elegant equipment of silver, ivory, gold. The bunks which lined all sides of the two rooms were nightly crowded and some of the people owned names which are not altogether unknown to the public. This place was raided because of sensational stories in the newspapers and the little wicket no longer opens to allow the anxious "fiend" to enter.

Upon the appearance of reform, opium retired to private flats. Here it now reigns and it will undoubtedly be an extremely long century before the police can root it from these little strongholds.

—Stephen Crane, American, 1871–1900

New York at Night, ca.1910. Louis Michel Eilshemius, American, 1864–1941.
Oil on cardboard, mounted on Masonite.
Bequest of Miss Adelaide Milton de Groot (1876–1967), 1967 67.187.158

LET US RAISE A STANDARD TO WHICH THE
WISE AND GOOD CAN REPAIR. THE REST IS
IN THE HANDS OF GOD.   WASHINGTON

from Willem de Kooning Remembers Mark Rothko

. . . it was in the Depression period. I had a studio in a loft on Twenty-second Street. So after a day's work I used to hang around Washington Square Park at night. Also we used to sit at the Waldorf Cafeteria. For years the artists had met there, you know, everybody. Rothko didn't come there very often. That's why I didn't know what he looked like. I had never met him. And so one night, in the park, it was late, wasn't a soul around. I walked around—thought I would sit a little bit on a bench. I was sitting way on the right side of the bench and kind of a husky man was on the left end of the bench, and I thought maybe I ought to move and sit on another bench. . . . I didn't know what he was thinking. We were just sitting there—wasn't a soul around. It must have been very late, or otherwise it was just one of those evenings that people didn't show up. And the park was really quite empty. And we just sat there until Mark said something like it was a nice evening. And so I said, "Yes, a nice evening," and we got to talk.

I guess he must have asked me what I did. I said, "I'm a painter." He says, "Oh, you're a painter? I'm a painter, too." And he said, "What's your name?" I said, "I'm Bill de Kooning." I said, "Who are you?" He says, "I'm Rothko." I said, "Oh, for God's sake," and said it was very funny. Then we talked, and a couple of days later he came to visit me in my studio.

—Willem de Kooning, American, 1904–1997

Chance Encounter at 3 A.M. (detail), 1984. Red Grooms, American, b. 1937. Oil on canvas. Purchase, Mr. and Mrs. Wolfgang Schoenborn Gift, 1984 1984.194

from **American Notes**

The great promenade and thoroughfare, as most people know, is Broadway; a wide and bustling street, which, from the Battery Gardens to its opposite termination in a country road, may be four miles long. Shall we sit down in an upper floor of the Carlton House Hotel (situated in the best part of this main artery of New York), and when we are tired of looking down upon the life below, sally forth arm-in-arm, and mingle with the stream?

Warm weather! The sun strikes upon our heads at this open window, as though its rays were concentrated through a burning-glass; but the day is in its zenith, and the season an unusual one. Was there ever such a sunny street as this Broadway? The pavement stones are polished with the tread of feet until they shine again; the red bricks of the houses might be yet in the dry, hot kilns; and the roofs of those omnibuses look as though, if water were poured on them, they would hiss and smoke, and smell like half-quenched fires. No stint of omnibuses here! Half-a-dozen have gone by within as many minutes.... Heaven save the ladies, how they dress! We have seen more colours in these ten minutes, than we should have seen elsewhere, in as many days. What various parasols! what rainbow silks and satins! what pinking of thin stockings, and pinching of thin shoes, and fluttering of ribbons and silk tassels, and display of rich cloaks with gaudy hoods and linings! The young gentlemen are fond, you see, of turning down their shirt-collars and cultivating their whiskers, especially under the chin; but they cannot approach the ladies in their dress or bearing, being, to say the truth, humanity of quite another sort.

—Charles Dickens, English, 1812–1870

New York from the Steeple of St. Paul's Church, looking East, South, and West, 1849. After John W. Hill, American, 1812–1879. Henry Papprill, active 1846–1850 (Engraver), Henry J. Megarey (Publisher). Aquatint with hand coloring, first state. The Edward W. C. Arnold Collection of New York Prints, Maps, and Pictures, Bequest of Edward W. C. Arnold, 1954 54.90.587

View of Central Park from a Room of the Dakota—Looking to Fifth Avenue, 1960s. Peter Fink, American, 1907–1984. Gelatin silver print. Purchase, Cournand Foundation Inc. Gift, 1965 65.681.7

from **Goodbye to All That**

...quite simply, I was in love with New York. I do not mean "love" in any colloquial way, I mean that I was in love with the city, the way you love the first person who ever touches you and never love anyone quite that way again. I remember walking across Sixty-second Street one twilight that first spring, or the second spring, they were all alike for a while. I was late to meet someone but I stopped at Lexington Avenue and bought a peach and stood on the corner eating it and knew that I had come out of the West and reached the mirage. I could taste the peach and feel the soft air blowing from a subway grating on my legs and I could smell lilac and garbage and expensive perfume and I knew that it would cost something sooner or later—because I did not belong there, did not come from there—but when you are twenty-two or twenty-three, you figure that later you will have a high emotional balance, and be able to pay whatever it costs. I still believed in possibilities then, still had the sense, so peculiar to New York, that something extraordinary would happen any minute, any day, any month. I was making only $65 or $70 a week then ("Put yourself in Hattie Carnegie's hands," I was advised without the slightest trace of irony by an editor of the magazine for which I worked), so little money that some weeks I had to charge food at Bloomingdale's gourmet shop in order to eat, a fact which went unmentioned in the letters I wrote to California. I never told my father that I needed money because then he would have sent it, and I would never know if I could do it by myself. At that time making a living seemed a game to me, with arbitrary but quite inflexible rules. And except on a certain kind of winter evening—six-thirty in the Seventies, say, already dark and bitter with a wind off the river, when I would be walking very fast toward a bus and would look in the bright windows of brownstones and see cooks working in clean kitchens and imagine women lighting candles on the floor above and beautiful children being bathed on the

floor above that—except
on nights like those, I
never felt poor; I had the
feeling that if I needed
money I could always get
it. I could write a syndi-
cated column for
teenagers under the name
"Debbi Lynn" or I could
smuggle gold into India or
I could become a $100
call girl, and none of it
would matter.

—Joan Didion, American,
b. 1934

East River Drive, 1976–77.
Yvonne Jacquette, American, b. 1934.
Pastel on paper.
Purchase, Friends of the Department
Gifts and matching funds from the
National Endowment for the Arts,
1978 1978.199

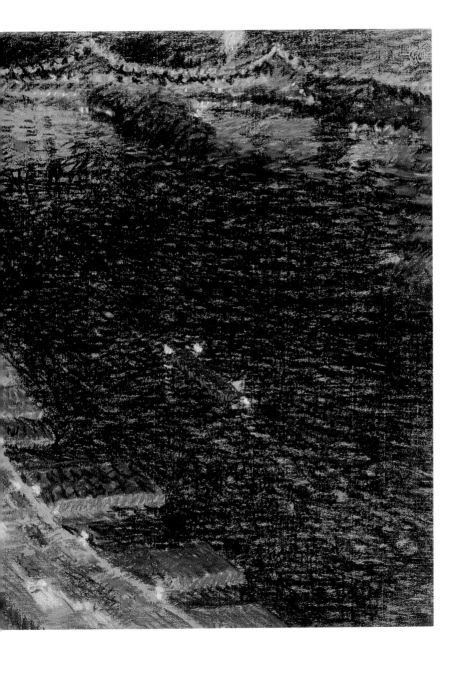

[Rivington Street], New York, N.Y., 1909.
Chromolithographic postcard published by the Detroit Publishing Co.
The Jefferson R. Burdick Collection, Gift of Jefferson R. Burdick (Album 416)

OVERLEAF: **From Williamsburg Bridge** (detail), 1928. Edward Hopper, American, 1882–1967.
Oil on canvas. George A. Hearn Fund, 1937 37.44

from **Ragtime**

People stitched themselves to the flag. They carved paving stones for the streets. They sang. They told jokes. The family lived in one room and everyone worked: Mameh, Tateh and The Little Girl in the pinafore. Mameh and the little girl sewed knee pants and got seventy cents a dozen. They sewed from the time they got up to the time they went to bed. Tateh made his living in the street. As time went on they got to know the city. One Sunday, in a wild impractical mood, they spent twelve cents for three fares on the streetcar and rode uptown. They walked on Madison Avenue and Fifth Avenue and looked at the mansions. Their owners called them palaces. And that's what they were, they were palaces. They had all been designed by Stanford White. Tateh was a socialist. He looked at the palaces and his heart was outraged. The family walked quickly. The police in their tall helmets looked at them. On these wide empty sidewalks in this part of the city the police did not like to see immigrants.

—E. L. Doctorow, American, b. 1931

from **Manhattan Transfer**

There are flags on all the flagpoles up Fifth Avenue. In the shrill wind
of history the great flags flap and tug at their lashings on the creaking
goldknobbed poles up Fifth Avenue. The stars jiggle sedately against the
slate sky, the red and white stripes writhe against the clouds.

    In the gale of brassbands and trampling horses and rumbling clat-
ter of cannon, shadows like the shadows of claws grasp at the taut flags,
the flags are hungry tongues licking twisting curling.

Oh it's a long way to Tipperary . . . Over there! Over there!

    The harbor is packed with zebrastriped skunkstriped piebald
steamboats, the Narrows are choked with bullion, they're piling gold
sovereigns up to the ceilings in the Subtreasury. Dollars whine on the
radio, all the cables tap out dollars.

There's a long long trail awinding . . . Over there! Over there!

    In the subway their eyes pop as they spell out APOCALYPSE, *typhus,*
cholera, shrapnel, insurrection, death in fire, death in water, death in
hunger, death in mud.

    Oh it's a long way to Madymosell from Armenteers, over there!
The Yanks are coming, the Yanks are coming. Down Fifth Avenue the
bands blare for the Liberty Loan drive, for the Red Cross drive.
Hospital ships sneak up the harbor and unload furtively at night in old
docks in Jersey. Up Fifth Avenue the flags of the seventeen nations are
flaring curling in the shrill hungry wind.

—John Dos Passos, American, 1896–1970

from The Great Gatsby

I began to like New York, the racy, adventurous feel of it at night and the satisfaction that the constant flicker of men and women and machines gives to the restless eye. I liked to walk up Fifth Avenue and pick out romantic women from the crowd and imagine that in a few minutes I was going to enter their lives, and no one would ever know or disapprove. Sometimes, in my mind, I followed them to their apartments on the corners of hidden streets, and they turned and smiled back at me before they faded through a door into warm darkness. At the enchanted metropolitan twilight I felt a haunting loneliness sometimes, and felt it in others—poor young clerks who loitered in front of windows waiting until it was time for a solitary restaurant dinner—young clerks in the dusk, wasting the most poignant moments of night and life.

Again at eight o' clock, when the dark lanes of the Forties were five deep with throbbing taxi cabs, bound for the theatre district, I felt a sinking in my heart. Forms leaned together in the taxis as they waited, and voices sang, and there was laughter from unheard jokes, and lighted cigarettes outlined unintelligible gestures inside. Imagining that I, too, was hurrying toward gayety and sharing their intimate excitement, I wished them well.

—F. Scott Fitzgerald, American, 1896–1940

from **Farewell**

Farewell to New York City, where twenty months have presented me with a richer and more varied exercise for thought and life than twenty years could in any other part of these United States.

It is the common remark about New-York that it has, at least, nothing petty or provincial in its methods and habits. The place is large enough; there is room enough and occupation enough for men to have no need or excuse for small cavils or scrutinies. A person who is independent and knows what he wants, may lead his proper life here unimpeded by others.

Vice and Crime, if flagrant and frequent, are less thickly coated by Hypocrisy than elsewhere. The air comes sometimes to the most infected subjects.

New-York is the focus, the point where American and European interests converge. There is no topic of general interest to men that will not betimes be brought before the thinker by the quick turning of the wheel.

—Margaret Fuller, American, 1810–1850

Union Park, New York (detail). Sarah Fairchild, American, active 1840s.
Watercolor, gouache, ink, and graphite on off-white wove paper.
Bequest of Edgar William and Bernice Chrysler Garbisch, 1979 1980.341.3

New York Blues

I live in an apartment, sink leaks thru the walls
Lower Eastside full of bedbugs. Junkies in the halls
House been broken into. Tibetan Tankas stole
Speed freaks took my statues, made my love a fool
   Speed freaks took my statues, made my love a fool

Days I came home tired nights I needed sleep
Cockroaches crawled in bed with me my brain began to creep
My work was never done, my rest'll never begin
I'll be dead and buried and never pleasure win
   I'll be dead and buried and never pleasure win

Lover boy threw meat at me cursed the day we met
Speed freaks and bedbugs New York City's what you get
Someday they'll build subways get rid of all the cars
Cops kill all the bedbugs speed freaks land on Mars
   Cops kill all the bedbugs speed freaks land on Mars

     —Allen Ginsberg, American, 1926–1997

The Battle of ABC, 1991. James Romberger, American, b. 1958.
Pastel on paper. Purchase, Dr. and Mrs. Robert E. Carroll Gift, 1991 1991.82

from **The New Yorkers**

Uptown on 125th Street is an old blind Black woman
she is out only in good
    weather and clothes
her house is probably spotless
as southern ladies are wont to keep house
and her wig is always on straight
    You got something for me, she called
    What do you want, I asked
    What's yo name? I know yo family
    No, you don't, I said laughing   You don't know anything
        about me
    You that Eyetalian poet ain't you? I know yo voice. I seen you
        on television
    I peered closely into her eyes
        You didn't see me or you'd know I'm black
        Let me feel yo hair   if you Black   Hold down yo head
    I did and she did
        Got something for me, she laughed
        You felt my hair   that's good luck
        Good luck is money, chile   she said
        Good luck is money

—Nikki Giovanni, American, b. 1943

Street Story Quilt (detail), 1985. Faith Ringgold, American, b. 1930.
Oil, felt-tip pen, dyed fabric, and sequins on canvas, sewn to quilted fabric.
Purchase, Arthur Hoppock Hearn Fund and funds from various donors, 1990 1990.237a–c

from **Manhattan**

Summer journeys
To Niag'ra
And to other places
Aggravate all our cares.
We'll save our fares.
I've a cozy little flat
In what is known as old Manhattan.
We'll settle down
Right here in town.

We'll have Manhattan,
The Bronx and Staten
Island too.
It's lovely going through
The zoo.
It's very fancy
On old Delancey
Street, you know.
The subway charms us so
When balmy breezes blow
To and fro.
And tell me what street
Compares with Mott Street
In July?
Sweet pushcarts gently gliding by.
The great big city's a wondrous toy
Just made for a girl and boy.

East River Panorama, ca. 1930, printed later. Samuel H. Gottscho, American, 1875–1971.
Gelatin silver print. Purchase, Florance Waterbury Bequest, 1970   1970.660.11

Couple at Coney Island, New York, 1928. Walker Evans, American, 1903–1975.
Gelatin silver print. Ford Motor Company Collection, Gift of Ford Motor Company and John C. Waddell, 1987
1987.1100.110

We'll turn Manhattan
Into an isle of joy. . . .

We'll go to Yonkers
Where true love conquers
In the wilds.
And starve together, dear,
In Childs'.
We'll go to Coney
And eat baloney
On a roll.
In Central Park we'll stroll,
Where our first kiss we stole,
Soul to soul.
Our future babies
We'll take to "Abie's
Irish Rose."
I hope they'll live to see
It close.
The city's clamor can never spoil
The dreams of a boy and goil.
We'll turn Manhattan
Into an isle of joy.

—Lorenz Hart, American, 1895–1943

from **The Mambo Kings Play Songs of Love**

. . . in those days it was a mark of sophistication among the Cubans of New York to speak English. At the parties they attended, given by Cubans all over the city, the better one's English, the higher his status. Conversing rapidly in Spanish, Cesar would offer proof of his linguistic facility by throwing in a phrase like "hep cats at a jam session." Now and then he fell in with a Greenwich Village crowd—American girls with bohemian spirits who would turn up at the Palladium or the Palm Nightclub; wild va-va-voom types who did not wear brassieres underneath their zebra-patterned party dresses. Meeting them on the dance floor, the Mambo King impressed them with his moves and Latin-lover mystique, and retired with them to their Village pads (with bathtubs in the kitchen) where they smoked reefers (he would feel a sugarcane field sprouting in his head), listened to bebop, and made out on dog-haired carpets and atop spring-worn couches. He picked up the words "jive" and "crazy!" (as in "Crazy, man, give me some skin!"), and with avuncular sexist tenderness lent them money and took them out to eat. In the period when he briefly went to work at the Tidy Print lithography plant on Chambers Street, to earn some extra money to buy a car, he would spend his lunch hours with this Jewish kid from Brooklyn, Bernardito Mandelbaum, teaching him Spanish. In the course of this he learned a few Yiddishisms. They'd trade words: *schlep* (dope), *schmuck* (fool), *schnook* (ignoramus), *schlemiel* (wastrel, fool), for *bobo* (dope), *vago* (lazy lout), *maricón* (fairy), and *pendejo* (ball-busting predatory louse). At some of these parties, where only English was spoken, he was famous for impressing even the driest Cuban professors with the exuberant variety of his speech.

—Oscar Hijuelos, American, b. 1951

El Morocco, 1955. Garry Winogrand, American, 1928–1984. Gelatin silver print.
Purchase, The Horace W. Goldsmith Foundation Gift, 1992 1992.5107

From the El, 1915. Paul Strand, American, 1890–1976.
Platinum print. Alfred Stieglitz Collection, 1949 49.55.221

from A Hazard of New Fortunes

At Third Avenue they took the elevated, for which she confessed an infat-
uation. She declared it the most ideal way of getting about in the world,
and was not ashamed when he reminded her of how she used to say that
nothing under the sun could induce her to travel on it. She now said that
the night transit was even more interesting than the day, and that the
fleeting intimacy you formed with people in second and third floor interi-
ors, while all the usual street life went on underneath, had a domestic
intensity mixed with a perfect repose that was the last effect of good soci-
ety with all its security and exclusiveness. He said it was better than the
theatre, of which it reminded him, to see those people through their windows: a family party of work-folk at a late tea, some of the men in their
shirt sleeves; a woman sewing by a lamp; a mother laying her child in its
cradle; a man with his head fallen on his hands upon a table; a girl and
her lover leaning over the window-sill together. What suggestion! what
drama! what infinite interest! At the Forty-second Street station they
stopped a minute on the bridge that crosses the track to the branch road
for the Central Depot, and looked up and down the long stretch of the
elevated to north and south. The track that found and lost itself a thousand times in the flare and tremor of the innumerable lights; the moony
sheen of the electrics mixing with the reddish points and blots of gas far
and near; the architectural shapes of houses and churches and towers,
rescued by the obscurity from all that was ignoble in them, and the coming and going of the trains marking the stations with vivider or fainter
plumes of flame-shot steam—formed an incomparable perspective. They
often talked afterward of the superb spectacle, which in a city full of
painters nightly works its unrecorded miracles. . . .

. . . she promised to write as soon as she reached home. She promised
also that having seen the limitations of New York in respect to flats, she

would not be hard on him if he took
something not quite ideal. Only he
must remember that it was not to be
above Twentieth Street nor below
Washington Square; it must not be
higher than the third floor; it must
have an elevator, steam heat, hall
boys, and a pleasant janitor. These
were essentials; if he could not get
them, then they must do without.
But he must get them.

—William Dean Howells, American,
1837–1920

Third Avenue, New York City, 1936. Remie Lohse,
American (b. Puerto Rico), 1892–1947.
Gelatin silver print. Ford Motor Company Collection,
Gift of Ford Motor Company and John C. Waddell,
1987 1987.1100.309

Juke Box Love Song

I could take the Harlem night
and wrap around you,
Take the neon lights and make a crown,
Take the Lenox Avenue busses,
Taxis, subways,
And for your love song tone their rumble down.
Take Harlem's heartbeat,
Make a drumbeat,
Put it on a record, let it whirl,
And while we listen to it play,
Dance with you till day—
Dance with you, my sweet brown Harlem girl.

Langston Hughes, American, 1902–1967

The **Block** (detail), 1971. Romare Bearden, American, 1911–1988.
Cut and pasted papers on Masonite.
Gift of Mr. and Mrs. Samuel Shore, 1978 1978.61.5

from **The Death and Life of Great American Cities**

The stretch of Hudson Street where I live is each day the scene of an intricate sidewalk ballet. I make my own first entrance into it a little after eight when I put out the garbage can, surely a prosaic occupation, but I enjoy my part, my little clang, as the droves of junior high school students walk by the center of the stage dropping candy wrappers. (How do they eat so much candy so early in the morning?)

While I sweep up the wrappers I watch the other rituals of morning: Mr. Halpert unlocking the laundry's handcart from its mooring to a cellar door, Joe Cornacchia's son-in-law stacking out the empty crates from the delicatessen, the barber bringing out his sidewalk folding chair, Mr. Goldstein arranging the coils of wire which proclaim the hardware store is open, the wife of the tenement's superintendent depositing her chunky three-year-old with a toy mandolin on the stoop, the vantage point from which he is learning the English his mother cannot speak. Now the primary children, heading for St. Luke's, dribble through to the south; the children for St. Veronica's cross, heading to the west, and the children for P.S. 41, heading toward the east. Two new entrances are being made from the wings: well-dressed and even elegant women and men with brief cases emerge from doorways and side streets. Most of these are heading for the bus and subways, but some hover on the curbs, stopping taxis which have miraculously appeared at the right moment, for the taxis are part of a wider morning ritual: having dropped passengers from midtown in the downtown financial district, they are now bringing downtowners up to midtown. Simultaneously, numbers of women in housedresses have

Greenwich Village Rooftops, Day, ca. 1952. André Kertész, American (b. Hungary), 1894–1985.
Gelatin silver print. Purchase, Rogers Fund, The Elisha Whittelsey Collection, The Elisha Whittelsey Fund,
and Mary Livingston Griggs and Mary Griggs Burke Foundation and Mrs. Vincent Astor Gifts, 1984.1083.18

Greenwich Village Rooftops, Evening, 1954. André Kertész, American (b. Hungary), 1894–1985.
Gelatin silver print. Purchase, Rogers Fund, The Elisha Whittelsey Collection, The Elisha Whittelsey Fund, and
Mary Livingston Griggs and Mary Griggs Burke Foundation and Mrs. Vincent Astor Gifts, 1984   1984.1083.28

emerged and as they crisscross with one another they pause for quick conversations that sound with either laughter or joint indignation, never, it seems, anything between. It is time for me to hurry to work too, and I exchange my ritual farewell with Mr. Lofaro, the short, thick-bodied, white-aproned fruit man who stands outside his doorway a little up the street, his arms folded, his feet planted, looking solid as earth itself. We nod; we each glance quickly up and down the street, then look back to each other and smile. We have done this many a morning for more than ten years, and we both know what it means: All is well.

—Jane Jacobs, American, b. 1916

from **Washington Square**

The ideal of quiet and of genteel retirement, in 1835, was found in
Washington Square, where the Doctor built himself a handsome, modern,
wide-fronted house, with a big balcony before the drawing-room windows,
and a flight of white marble steps ascending to a portal which was also faced
with white marble. This structure, and many of its neighbors, which it exactly resembled, were supposed, forty years ago, to embody the last results of
architectural science, and they remain to this day very solid and honorable
dwellings. In front of them was the Square, containing a considerable quan-
tity of inexpensive vegetation, enclosed by a wooden paling, which increased
its rural and accessible appearance; and round the corner was the more
august precinct of the Fifth Avenue, taking its origin at this point with a spa-
cious and confident air which already marked it for high destinies. I know
not whether it is owing to the tenderness of early associations, but this portion of New York appears to many persons the most delectable. It has a kind
of established repose which is not a frequent occurrence in other quarters of
the long, shrill city; it has a riper, richer, more honorable look than any of
the upper ramifications of the great longitudinal thoroughfare—the look of
having had something of a social history.

—Henry James, American, 1843–1916

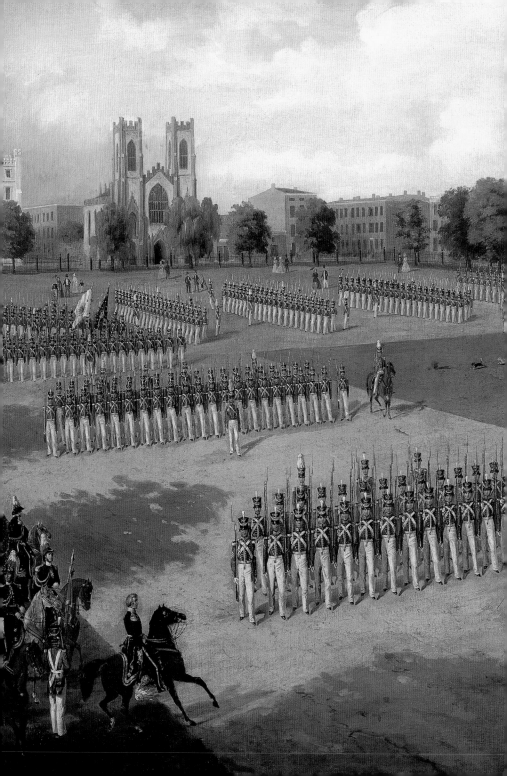

City of Ambition, 1910, printed ca. 1913. Alfred Stieglitz, American, 1864–1946.
Photogravure. Alfred Stieglitz Collection, 1949 49.55.15

from The Autobiography of an Ex-colored Man

We steamed up into New York Harbor late one afternoon in spring. The last efforts of the sun were being put forth in turning the waters of the bay to glistening gold; the green islands on either side, in spite of their warlike mountings, looked calm and peaceful; the buildings of the town shone out in a reflected light which gave the city an air of enchantment; and, truly, it is an enchanted spot. New York City is the most fatally fascinating thing in America. She sits like a great witch at the gate of the country, showing her alluring white face and hiding her crooked hands and feet under the folds of her wide garments—constantly enticing thousands from far within, and tempting those who come from across the seas to go no farther. And all these become the victims of her caprice. Some she at once crushes beneath her cruel feet; others she condemns to a fate like that of galley-slaves; a few she favors and fondles, riding them high on the bubbles of fortune; then with a sudden breath she blows the bubbles out and laughs mockingly as she watches them fall.

Twice I had passed through it, but this was really my first visit to New York; and as I walked about that evening, I began to feel the dread power of the city; the crowds, the lights, the excitement, the gaiety, and all its subtler stimulating influences began to take effect upon me. My blood ran quicker and I felt that I was just beginning to live. To some natures this stimulant of life in a great city becomes a thing as binding and necessary as opium is to one addicted to the habit. It becomes their breath of life; they cannot exist outside of it; rather than be deprived of it they are content to suffer hunger, want, pain, and misery; they would not exchange even a ragged and wretched condition among the great crowd for any degree of comfort away from it.

—James Weldon Johnson, American, 1871–1938

from **New York Jew**

The next morning I went as usual to my office. It was a brilliantly clear day, and usually it was impossible in that office, overlooking the heaped-up splendor of New York, to feel oneself less than brilliant. It was from working in that building that I knew why every sentence in *Time* had to strike like a rapier, shine like steel. The rows of metal desks glistened in the light. Brilliantly resourceful girls—researchers, who were not allowed to write—walked back and forth on editorial errands to their writers. Early as it was, one writer a cubicle away from me could already be heard chanting to himself from the Bhagavad-Gita. Another was sending out to the hall on his portable phonograph the allegretto from Beethoven's Seventh. The old boys were coming in from Ossining and Greenwich and Stamford with their impressively scuffed English attaché cases, saying witty doomsday things to each other, like characters in a John Cheever story, about the daily disasters of country living. Down in the concourse, where the city mob flowing out into the Fiftieth Street station of the Independent met the tourists with circular tickets around their necks looking with awe at every last wonder in Rockefeller Center, the chromium and steel frames around the window glass glistened more brightly than ever while on the wings of light itself messages sped from the cable center to every corner of the world. And I was part of it all. . . .

—Alfred Kazin, American, 1915–1998

Rockefeller Center, ca. 1936. Wendell MacRae, American, 1896–1980.
Gelatin silver print. Purchase, David Hunter McAlpin Fund and matching funds from
the National Endowment for the Arts, 1980 1980.1116.1

Port Authority (detail), 1966–67. Ray Metzker, American, b. 1931.
Composite of twelve gelatin silver prints. Purchase, Stewart S. MacDermott Fund,
Nancy and Edwin Marks Gift, Mary Martin Fund, Joyce and Robert Menschel Gift,
and The Horace W. Goldsmith Foundation Gift, 1990 1990.1083

from **On the Road**

Suddenly I found myself on Times Square. I had traveled eight thousand
miles around the American continent and I was back on Times Square; and
right in the middle of a rush hour, too, seeing with my innocent road-eyes
the absolute madness and fantastic hoorair of New York with its millions and
millions hustling forever for a buck among themselves, the mad dream—
grabbing, taking, giving, sighing, dying, just so they could be buried in those
awful cemetery cities beyond Long Island City. The high towers of the
land—the other end of the land, the place where Paper America is born. I
stood in a subway doorway, trying to get enough nerve to pick up a beautiful
long butt, and every time I stooped great crowds rushed by and obliterated
it from my sight, and finally it was crushed. I had no money to go home in
the bus. Paterson is quite a few miles from Times Square. Can you picture
me walking those last miles through the Lincoln Tunnel or over the
Washington Bridge and into New Jersey? It was dusk. Where was Hassel? I
dug the square for Hassel; he wasn't there, he was in Riker's Island, behind
bars. Where Dean? Where everybody? Where life? I had my home to go to,
my place to lay my head down and figure the losses and figure the gain that
I knew was in there somewhere too. I had to panhandle two bits for the bus.
I finally hit a Greek minister who was standing around the corner. He gave
me the quarter with a nervous lookaway. I rushed immediately to the bus.

—Jack Kerouac, American, 1922–1969

The New Colossus

Not like the brazen giant of Greek fame,
With conquering limbs astride from land to land;
Here at our sea-washed, sunset gates shall stand
A mighty woman with a torch, whose flame
Is the imprisoned lightning, and her name
Mother of Exiles. From her beacon-hand
Glows world-wide welcome; her mild eyes command
The air-bridged harbor that twin cities frame.
"Keep, ancient lands, your storied pomp!" cries she
With silent lips. "Give me your tired, your poor,
Your huddled masses yearning to breathe free,
The wretched refuse of your teeming shore.
Send these, the homeless, tempest-tost to me,
I lift my lamp beside the golden door!"

—Emma Lazarus, American, 1849–1887

The Statue of Liberty, New York Harbor (detail), 1905
Chromolithographic postcard published by the Detroit Publishing Co.
The Jefferson R. Burdick Collection, Gift of Jefferson R. Burdick Album 416

Fourteenth Street, 1990. Per Bak Jensen, Danish, b. 1949.
Gelatin silver print. Gift of the artist, 1991 1991.1145

from The City in Which I Love You

Morning comes to this city vacant of you.
Pages and windows flare, and you are not there.
Someone sweeps his portion of sidewalk,
wakens the drunk, slumped like laundry,
and you are gone.

You are not in the wind
which someone notes in the margins of a book.
You are gone out of the small fires in abandoned lots
where human figures huddle,
each aspiring to its own ghost.

Between brick walls, in a space no wider than my face,
a leafless sapling stands in mud.
In its branches, a nest of raw mouths
gaping and cheeping, scrawny fires that must eat.
My hunger for you is no less than theirs.

—Li-Young Lee, American, b. 1957

from The Group

It was June, 1933, one week after Commencement, when Kay Leiland Strong, Vassar '33, the first of her class to run around the table at the Class Day dinner, was married to Harald Petersen, Reed '27, in the chapel of St. George's Church, P.E., Karl F. Reiland, Rector. Outside, on Stuyvesant Square, the trees were in full leaf, and the wedding guests arriving by twos and threes in taxis heard the voices of children playing round the statue of Peter Stuyvesant in the park. Paying the driver, smoothing out their gloves, the pairs and trios of young women, Kay's classmates, stared about them curiously, as though they were in a foreign city. They were in the throes of discovering New York, imagine it, when some of them had actually lived here all their lives, in tiresome Georgian houses full of waste space in the Eighties or Park Avenue apartment buildings, and they delighted in such out-of-the-way corners as this, with its greenery and Quaker meeting-house in red brick, polished brass, and white trim next to the wine-purple Episcopal church—on Sundays, they walked with their beaux across Brooklyn Bridge and poked into the sleepy Heights section of Brooklyn; they explored residential Murray Hill and quaint MacDougal Alley and Patchin Place and Washington Mews with all the artists' studios; they loved the Plaza Hotel and the fountain there and the green mansarding of the Savoy Plaza and the row of horsedrawn hacks and elderly coachmen, waiting, as in a French *place*, to tempt them to a twilight right through Central Park.

—Mary McCarthy, American, 1912–1989

Spring in Central Park (detail), 1941. Adolf Dehn, American, 1895–1968.
Watercolor on paper. Fletcher Fund, 1941 41.113ab

United States Army Bomber in Flight over New York City, ca. 1938. Wendell MacRae, American, 1896–1980. Gelatin silver print. Purchase, Lila Acheson Wallace Gift, 1983 1983.1189.8

Recuerdo

We were very tired, we were very merry—
We had gone back and forth all night on the ferry.
It was bare and bright, and smelled like a stable—
But we looked into a fire, we leaned across a table,
We lay on a hill-top underneath the moon;
And the whistles kept blowing, and the dawn came soon.

We were very tired, we were very merry—
We had gone back and forth all night on the ferry;
And you ate an apple, and I ate a pear,
From a dozen of each we had bought somewhere;
And the sky went wan, and the wind came cold,
And the sun rose dripping, a bucketful of gold.

We were very tired, we were very merry,
We had gone back and forth all night on the ferry.
We hailed, "Good morrow, mother!" to a shawl-covered head,
And bought a morning paper, which neither of us read;
And she wept, "God bless you!" for the apples and pears,
And we gave her all our money but our subway fares.

—Edna St. Vincent Millay, American, 1892–1950

From a New York Ferryboat, 1904. Joseph T. Keiley, American, 1869–1914. Platinum print. Alfred Stieglitz Collection, 1933 33.43.178

Riverside Park Near 153rd Street, 1944. André Kertész, American (b. Hungary), 1894–1985.
Gelatin silver print. Purchase, Rogers Fund, The Elisha Whittelsey Collection, The Elisha Whittelsey Fund, and
Mary Livingston Griggs and Mary Griggs Burke Foundation and Mrs. Vincent Astor Gifts, 1984 1984.1083.40

from **The Rivermen**

I often feel drawn to the Hudson River, and I have spent a lot of time
through the years poking around the part of it that flows past the city. I never
get tired of looking at it; it hypnotizes me. I like to look at it in midsummer,
when it is warm and dirty and drowsy, and I like to look at it in January, when
it is carrying ice. I like to look at when it is stirred up, when a northeast
wind is blowing and a strong tide is running—a new-moon tide or a full-
moon tide—and I like to look at it when it is slack. It is exciting to me on
weekdays, when it is crowded with ocean craft, harbor craft, and river craft,
but it is the river itself that draws me, and not the shipping, and I guess I like
it best on Sundays, when there are lulls that sometimes last as long as half an
hour, during which, all the way from the Battery to the George Washington
Bridge, nothing moves upon it, not even a ferry, not even a tug, and it
becomes as hushed and dark and secret and remote and unreal as a river in a
dream. Once, in the course of such a lull, on a Sunday morning in April,
1950, I saw a sea sturgeon rise out of the water. I was on the New Jersey side
of the river that morning, sitting in the sun on an Erie Railroad coal dock. I
knew that every spring a few sturgeon still come in from the sea and go up
the river to spawn, as hundreds of thousands of them once did, and I had
heard tugboatmen talk about them, but this was the first one I had ever seen.
It was six or seven feet long, a big, full-grown sturgeon. It rose twice, and
cleared the water both times, and I plainly saw its bristly snout and its shiny
little eyes and its white belly and its glistening, greenish-yellow, bony-plated,
crocodilian back and sides, and it was a spooky sight.

—Joseph Mitchell, American, 1908–1996

from Jazz

I'm crazy about this City.

Daylight slants like a razor cutting the buildings in half. In the top half I see looking faces and it's not easy to tell which are people, which the work of stonemasons. Below is shadow where any blasé thing takes place: clarinets and lovemaking, fists and the voices of sorrowful women. A city like this one makes me dream tall and feel in on things. Hep. It's the bright steel rocking above the shade below that does it. When I look over strips of green grass lining the river, at church steeples and into the cream-and-copper halls of apartment buildings, I'm strong. Alone, yes, but top-notch and indestructible—like the City in 1926 when all the wars are over and there will never be another one. The people down there in the shadow are happy about that. At last, at last, everything's ahead. The smart ones say so and people listening to them and reading what they write down agree: Here comes the new. Look out. There goes the sad stuff. The bad stuff. The things-nobody-could-help stuff. The way everybody was then and there. Forget that. History is over, you all, and everything's ahead at last.

—Toni Morrison, American, b. 1931

Manhattan Temple—B.C. Lunch, 1936. James VanDerZee, American, 1886–1983.
Gelatin silver print. Gift of James VanDerZee Institute, 1970   1970.539.53

OVERLEAF: **42nd Street**, 1929. Walker Evans, American, 1903–1975.
Gelatin silver print. Ford Motor Company Collection, Gift of Ford Motor Company and
John C. Waddell, 1987   1987.1100.68

Two Towers–New York, ca. 1910–13, printed ca. 1913. Alfred Stieglitz, American, 1864–1946. Photogravure. Alfred Stieglitz Collection, 1949 49.55.19

I Want New York

I think those people are utterly unreliable
Who say they'd be happy on a desert island with a copy of the Biable
And Hamlet (by Shakespeare) and Don Quixote (by Cervantes)
And poems by Homer and Virgil and perhaps a thing or two of Dante's.
And furthermore, I have a feeling that if they were marooned till the
millennium's dawn
Very few of us would notice that they were gone.
Perhaps they don't like my opinions any better than I like theirs,
But who cares?
If I were going to be marooned and could take only one thing along
I'd be perfectly happy if I could take the thing which is the subject of
this song.
I don't mean anything that was brought either by the postman or the stork.
I mean the City of New York.
For New York is a wonder city, a veritable fairyland
With many sights not to be seen in Massachusetts or Maryland.
It is situated on the island of Manhattan
Which I prefer to such islands as Welfare or Staten.
And it is far superior
To the cities of the interior.
What if it has a heterogeneous populace?
That is one of the privileges of being a metropulace
And heterogeneous people don't go around bothering each other
And you can be reasonably sure that everything you do won't get right back
to your dear old mother.
In New York beautiful girls can become more beautiful by going to
Elizabeth Arden
And getting stuff put on their faces and waiting for it to harden

And poor girls with nothing to their names but a letter or two can get rich and joyous

From a brief trip to their loyous.

And anybody with a relative of whose will he is the beneficiary

Can do pretty well in the judiciary.

So I can say with impunity

That New York is a city of opportunity.

It also has many fine theaters and hotels,

And a lot of taxis, buses, subways and els,

Best of all, if you don't show up at the office or at a tea nobody will bother their head

They will just think you are dead.

That's why I really think New York is exquisite.

It isn't all right just for a visit

But by God's Grace

I'd live in it and like it even better if you gave me the place.

—Ogden Nash, American, 1902–1971

Empire State Building Under Construction, 1931. Wendell MacRae, American, 1896–1980.
Gelatin silver print. Purchase, David Hunter McAlpin Fund and matching funds from
the National Endowment for the Arts, 1980 1980.1116.5

Steps

How funny you are today New York
like Ginger Rogers in *Swingtime*
and St. Bridget's steeple leaning a little to the left

here I have just jumped out of a bed full of V-days
(I got tired of D-days) and blue you there still
accepts me foolish and free
all I want is a room up there
and you in it
and even the traffic halt so thick is a way
for people to rub up against each other
and when their surgical appliances lock
they stay together
for the rest of the day (what a day)
I go by to check a slide and I say
that painting's not so blue

where's Lana Turner
she's out eating
and Garbo's backstage at the Met
everyone's taking their coat off
so they can show a rib-cage to the rib-watchers
and the park's full of dancers and their tights and shoes
in little bags

who are often mistaken for worker-outers at the West Side Y
why not
the Pittsburgh Pirates shout because they won
and in a sense we're all winning
we're alive

the apartment was vacated by a gay couple
who moved to the country for fun
they moved a day too soon
even the stabbings are helping the population explosion
though in the wrong country
and all those liars have left the U N
the Seagram Building's no longer rivalled in interest
not that we need liquor (we just like it)

and the little box is out on the sidewalk
next to the delicatessen
so the old man can sit on it and drink beer
and get knocked off it by his wife later in the day
while the sun is still shining

oh god it's wonderful
to get out of bed
and drink too much coffee
and smoke too many cigarettes
and love you so much

—Frank O'Hara, American, 1926–1966

"Lullaby of Broadway" from **"The Gold Diggers of 1935,"** 1935. Unknown artist, American school.
Gelatin silver print. Ford Motor Company Collection, Gift of Ford Motor Company
and John C. Waddell, 1987 1987.1100.142

from **An Unfinished Story**

Dulcie worked in a department store. She sold Hamburg edging, or stuffed peppers, or automobiles, or other little trinkets such as they keep in department stores. Of what she earned, Dulcie received six dollars per week. . . .

One afternoon at six, when Dulcie was sticking her hat pin within an eighth of an inch of her *medulla oblongata*, she said to her chum, Sadie—the girl that waits on you with her left side:

"Say, Sade, I made a date for dinner this evening with Piggy."

"You never did!" exclaimed Sadie, admiringly. "Well, ain't you the lucky one? Piggy's an awful swell; and he always takes a girl to swell places. He took Blanche up to the Hoffman House one evening, where they have swell music, and you see a lot of swells. You'll have a swell time, Dulce."

Dulcie hurried homeward. Her eyes were shining, and her cheeks showed the delicate pink of life's—real life's—approaching dawn. It was Friday; and she had fifty cents left of her last week's wages.

The streets were filled with the rush-hour floods of people. The electric lights of Broadway were glowing—calling moths from miles, from leagues, from hundreds of leagues out of darkness around to come in and attend the singeing school. Men in accurate clothes, with faces like those carved on cherry stones by the old salts in sailors' homes, turned and stared at Dulcie as she sped, unheeding, past them. Manhattan, the night-blooming cereus, was beginning to unfold its dead-white, heavy-odored petals.

—O. Henry, American, 1862–1910

Broadway and 42nd Street (detail), 1902. Childe Hassam, American, 1859–1935.
Oil on canvas. Bequest of Miss Adelaide Milton de Groot (1876–1967), 1967 67.187.128

from A Letter to
The Columbia Spy, May 27, 1844

When you visit Gotham, you should ride out the Fifth Avenue, as far as the distributing reservoir, near Forty-third Street, I believe. The prospect from the walk around the reservoir is particularly beautiful. You can see, from this elevation, the north reservoir at Yorkville; the whole city to the Battery; with a large portion of the harbor, and long reaches of the Hudson and East rivers. Perhaps even a finer view, however, is to be obtained from the summit of the white, light-house-looking shot-tower which stands on the East river, at Fifty-fifth Street, or thereabouts.

A day or two since I procured a light skiff, and with the aid of a pair of *sculls* (as they here term short oars, or paddles) made my way around Blackwell's Island, on a voyage of discovery and exploration. The chief interest of the adventure lay in the scenery of the Manhattan shore, which is here particularly picturesque. The houses are, without exception, *frame*, and antique. Nothing very modern has been attempted—a necessary result of the subdivision of the whole island into streets and town-lots. I could not look on the magnificent cliffs, and stately trees, which at every moment met my view, without a sigh for their inevitable doom—inevitable and swift. In twenty years, or thirty at farthest, we shall see here nothing more romantic than shipping, warehouses, and wharves.

—Edgar Allan Poe, American, 1809–1849

View of South Street, from Maiden Lane, New York City (detail), 1828. William James Bennett, British (active in New York), 1787–1844. Watercolor and pen and ink on off-white wove paper. The Edward W. C. Arnold Collection of New York Prints, Maps, and Pictures, Bequest of Edward W. C. Arnold, 1954 54.90.130

OVERLEAF: New York from Brooklyn Heights, 1837. William James Bennett, British (active in New York), 1787–1844, after John W. Hill, American, 1812–1879. Etching and aquatint with handcoloring. The Edward W. C. Arnold Collection of New York Prints, Maps, and Pictures, Bequest of Edward W. C. Arnold, 1954 54.90.586

The Octopus, 1912. Alvin Langdon Coburn, British (b. United States), 1882–1966.
Platinum print. Ford Motor Company Collection, Gift of Ford Motor Company and
John C. Waddell, 1987 1987.1100.13

OVERLEAF: Metropolitan Tower, 1912. Guy C. Wiggins, American, 1883–1962.
Oil on canvas. George A. Hearn Fund, 1912 12.105.4

N.Y.

My City, my beloved, my white! Ah, slender,
Listen! Listen to me, and I will breathe into thee a soul.
Delicately upon the reed, attend me!

Now do I know that I am mad,
For here are a million people surly with traffic;
This is no maid.
Neither could I play upon any reed if I had one.

My City, my beloved,
Thou art a maid with no breasts,
Thou art slender as a silver reed.
Listen to me, attend me!
And I will breathe into thee a soul,
And thou shalt live for ever.

—Ezra Pound, American, 1885–1972

[Corner of Bowery and Grand], 1932, printed 1980s. Leo Brooks, American.
Gelatin silver print. Gift of Woody Brooks, 1988   1988.1106.1

from **How the Other Half Lives**

The metropolis is to lots of people like a lighted candle to the moth. It attracts them in swarms that come year after year with the vague idea that they can get along here if anywhere; that something is bound to turn up among so many. Nearly all are young men, unsettled in life, many—most of them, perhaps—fresh from good homes, beyond a doubt with honest hopes of getting a start in the city and making a way for themselves. Few of them have much money to waste while looking around, and the cheapness of the lodging offered is an object. Fewer still know anything about the city and its pitfalls. They have come in search of crowds, of "life," and they gravitate naturally to the Bowery, the great democratic highway of the city, where the twenty-five cent lodging-houses take them in. In the alleged reading-rooms of these great barracks, that often have accommodations, such as they are, for two, three, and even four hundred guests, they encounter three distinct classes of associates: the great mass adventurers like themselves, waiting there for something to turn up; a much smaller class of respectable clerks or mechanics, who, too poor or too lonely to have a home of their own, live this way from year to year; and lastly the thief in search of recruits for his trade. The sights the young stranger sees, and the company he keeps, in the Bowery are not of a kind to strengthen any moral principle he may have brought away from home, and by the time his money is gone, with no work yet in sight, and he goes down a step, a long step, to the fifteen-cent lodg-ing-house, he is ready for the tempter whom he finds waiting for him there, reinforced by the contingent of ex-convicts returning from the prisons after having served out their sentences for robbery or theft. Then it is that the something he has been waiting for turns up. The police returns have the record of it.

—Jacob Riis, American, 1849–1914

East River from the Shelton, 1928. Georgia O'Keeffe, American, 1887–1986.
Oil on canvas. Alfred Stieglitz Collection, Bequest of Georgia O'Keeffe, 1986 1987.377.3

Times Square, ca. 1938, printed later. Rudolf Burckhardt, American (b. Switzerland), 1914–1999.
Gelatin silver print. Gift of Weston J. Naef, 1983   1983.1164

from **The Bloodhounds of Broadway**

One morning along about four bells, I am standing in front of Mindy's restaurant on Broadway with a guy by the name of Regret, who has this name because it seems he wins a very large bet the year the Whitney filly, Regret, grabs the Kentucky Derby, and can never forget it, which is maybe because it is the only very large bet he ever wins in his life.

What this guy's real name is I never hear, and anyway names make no difference to me, especially on Broadway, because the chances are that no matter what name a guy has, it is not his square name. . . .

It is generally pretty quiet on Broadway along about four bells in the morning, because at such an hour the citizens are mostly in speakeasies, and night clubs, and on this morning I am talking about it is very quiet, indeed, except for a guy by the name of Marvin Clay hollering at a young doll because she will not get into a taxicab with him to go to his apartment. But of course Regret and I do not pay much attention to such a scene, except that Regret remarks that the young doll seems to have more sense than you will expect to see in a doll loose on Broadway at four bells in the morning, because it is well known to one and all that any doll who goes to Marvin Clay's apartment, either has no brains whatever, or wishes to go there.

—Damon Runyon, American, 1884–1946

Trinity Place

The grave of Alexander Hamilton is in Trinity yard at the end of Wall Street.

The grave of Robert Fulton likewise is in Trinity yard where Wall Street stops.

And in this yard stenogs, bundle boys, scrubwomen, sit on the tombstones,
and walk on the grass of graves, speaking of war and weather, of babies,
wages and love.

An iron picket fence . . . and streaming thousands along Broadway sidewalks
. . . straw hats, faces, legs . . . a singing, talking, hustling river . . . down
the great street that ends with a Sea.

. . . easy is the sleep of Alexander Hamilton.
. . . easy is the sleep of Robert Fulton.
. . . easy are the great governments and the great steamboats.

—Carl Sandburg, American, 1878–1967

Wall Street, 1920s. Sherril Schell, American, 1877–1964.
Gelatin silver print. David Hunter McAlpin Fund, 1963 63.500.6

[Empire State Building Above Brownstone Buildings], 1920s–30s.
Herbert J. Seligmann, American, 1891–1984. Gelatin silver print. Ford Motor Company Collection,
Gift of Ford Motor Company and John C. Waddell, 1987   1987.1100.473

Wonderful World

for Anne Waldman
July 23, 1969

"I," I mused, "yes, I," and turned to the fenestrations of the night beyond
one of Ada and Alex Katz's windows. Deep in Prince Street lurked thin
sullen fumes of Paris green; some great spotty Danes moved from room to
room, their tails went whack whack in a kindly way and their mouths were
full of ruses (roses). Flames in red glass pots, unlikely flowers, a spot of light
that jumped ("Don't fret") back and forth over a strip of moulding, the kind
of moulding that spells low class dwelling—I, I mused, take no interest in
the distinction between amateur and pro, and despise the latter a little less
each year. The spot of light, reflected off a cup of strong blue coffee, wasn't
getting anywhere but it wasn't standing still. They say a lot of gangsters'
mothers live around here, so the streets are safe. A vast and distant school
building made chewing noises in its sleep. Our Lady of someplace stood up
in a wood niche with lots and lots of dollar bills pinned around her. The
night was hot, everybody went out in the street and sold each other hot
sausages and puffy sugared farinaceous products fried in deep fat ("Don't
put your fingers in that, dear") while the band played and the lady in the silver fox scarf with the beautiful big crack in her voice sang about the young
man and how he ran out in front of the stock exchange and drank a bottle of
household ammonia: "Ungrateful Heart." Big rolls of paper were delivered,
tall spools of thread spun and spelled Jacquard, Jacquard. Collecting the
night in her hand, rolling its filaments in a soft ball, Anne said, "I grew up
around here," where, looking uptown on summer evenings, the Empire
State Building rears its pearly height.

—James Schuyler, American, 1923–1991

from **Enemies, A Love Story**

Herman's office was in a building on Twenty-third Street near Fourth Avenue. He could get to the subway at Stillwell Avenue by walking down Mermaid, Neptune, or Surf Avenues, or by the Boardwalk. Each of these routes had its attractions, but today he chose Mermaid Avenue. This street had an Eastern European flavor. Last year's posters announcing cantors and rabbis and the prices of synagogue pews for the High Holy Days still hung on the walls. From the restaurants and cafeterias came the smells of chicken soup, kasha, chopped liver. The bakeries sold bagels and egg cookies, strudel and onion rolls. In front of a shop, women were groping in barrels for dill pickles.

Even if he never had had a large appetite, the hunger of the Nazi years had left Herman with a sense of excitement at the sight of food. Sunlight fell on crates and bushel baskets of oranges, bananas, cherries, strawberries, and tomatoes. Jews were allowed to live freely here! On the main avenue and on the side streets, Hebrew schools displayed their signs. There was even a Yiddish school. As Herman walked along, his eye sought hiding places in case the Nazis were to come to New York. Could a bunker be dug somewhere nearby? Could he hide himself in the steeple of the Catholic church? He had never been a partisan, but now he often thought of positions from which it would be possible to shoot.

On Stillwell Avenue, Herman turned right, and the hot wind struck him with the sweet smell of popcorn. Barkers urged people into amusement parks and side shows. There were carousels, shooting galleries, mediums who would conjure the spirits of the dead for fifty cents. At the subway entrance, a puffy-eyed Italian was banging a long knife against an iron bar, calling out a single word again and again, in a voice that carried over all the tumult. He was selling cotton candy and soft ice cream that melted as soon as it was put into a cone. On the other side of the

Coney Island, 1947. Sid Grossman, American, 1915–1955.
Gelatin silver print. Purchase, The Horace W. Goldsmith Foundation Gift, 1986 1986.1023

Boardwalk, the ocean sparkled beyond a swarm of bodies. The richness of color, the abundance, the freedom— cheap and shoddy as everything was— surprised Herman each time he saw it.

—Isaac Bashevis Singer, American, 1904–1991
translation Aliza Shevrin and Elizabeth Shub

Steeplechase, Coney Island, 1929. Milton Avery, American, 1885–1965. Oil on canvas. Gift of Sally M. Avery, 1984 1984.527

from **A Tree Grows in Brooklyn**

Serene was a word you could put to Brooklyn, New York. Especially in the summer of 1912. Somber, as a word, was better. But it did not apply to Williamsburg, Brooklyn. Prairie was lovely and Shenandoah had a beautiful sound, but you couldn't fit those words into Brooklyn. Serene was the only word for it; especially on a Saturday afternoon in summer.

Late in the afternoon the sun slanted down into the mossy yard belonging to Francie Nolan's house, and warmed the worn wooden fence. Looking at the shafted sun, Francie had that same fine feeling that came when she recalled the poem they recited in school.

> This is the forest primeval. The murmuring pines and the hemlocks,
> Bearded with moss, and in garments green, indistinct in the twilight,
> Stand like Druids of eld.

The one tree in Francie's yard was neither a pine nor a hemlock. It had pointed leaves which grew along green switches which radiated from the bough and made a tree like a lot of opened green umbrellas. Some people called it the Tree of Heaven. No matter where its seed fell, it made a tree which struggled to reach the sky. It grew in boarded-up lots and out of neglected rubbish heaps and it was the only tree that grew out of cement. It grew lushly, but only in the tenement districts.

You took a walk on a Sunday afternoon and came to a nice neighborhood, very refined. You saw a small one of these trees through the iron gate leading to someone's yard and you knew that soon that section of Brooklyn would get to be a tenement district. The tree knew. It came there first.

—Betty Smith, American, 1904–1972

Backyards, Brooklyn (detail), 1932. Ogden M. Pleissner, American, 1905–1983. Oil on canvas. Arthur Hoppock Hearn Fund, 1932 32.80.2

The Street—Winter, 1897, printed ca. 1913. Alfred Stieglitz, American, 1864–1946.
Photogravure. Alfred Stieglitz Collection, 1949 49.55.8

from The Age of Innocence

On a January evening of the early seventies, Christine Nilsson was singing in *Faust* at the Academy of Music in New York.

Though there was already talk of the erection, in remote metropolitan distances "above the Forties," of a new Opera House which should compete in costliness and splendour with those of the great European capitals, the world of fashion was still content to reassemble every winter in the shabby red and gold boxes of the sociable old Academy. Conservatives cherished it for being small and inconvenient, and thus keeping out the "new people" whom New York was beginning to dread and yet be drawn to; and the sentimental clung to it for its historic associations, and the musical for its excellent acoustics, always so problematic a quality in halls built for the hearing of music. . . .

When Newland Archer opened the door at the back of the club box the curtain had just gone up on the garden scene. There was no reason why the young man should not have come earlier, for he had dined at seven, alone with his mother and sister, and had lingered afterward over a cigar in the Gothic library with glazed black-walnut bookcases and finial-topped chairs, which was the only room in the house where Mrs. Archer allowed smoking. But, in the first place, New York was a metropolis, and perfectly aware that in metropolises it was "not the thing" to arrive early at the opera; and what was or was not "the thing" played a part as important in Newland Archer's New York as the inscrutable totem terrors that had ruled the destinies of his forefathers thousands of years ago.

—Edith Wharton, American, 1862–1937

from Here Is New York

There are roughly three New Yorks. There is, first, the New York of the man or woman who was born here, who takes the city for granted and accepts its size and its turbulence as natural and inevitable. Second, there is the New York of the commuter—the city that is devoured by locusts each day and spat out each night. Third, there is the New York of the person who was born somewhere else and came to New York in quest of something. Of these three trembling cities the greatest is the last—the city of final destination, the city that is a goal. It is this third city that accounts for New York's high-strung disposition, its poetical deportment, its dedication to the arts, and its incomparable achievements. Commuters give the city its tidal restlessness; natives give it solidity and continuity; but the settlers give it passion. And whether it is a farmer arriving from Italy to set up a small grocery store in a slum, or a young girl arriving from a small town in Mississippi to escape the indignity of being observed by her neighbors, or a boy arriving from the Corn Belt with a manuscript in his suitcase and a pain in his heart, it makes no difference: each embraces New York with the intense excitement of first love, each absorbs New York with the fresh eyes of an adventurer, each generates heat and light to dwarf the Consolidated Edison Company.

—E. B. White, American, 1899–1985

Untitled Film Still #21, 1978. Cindy Sherman, American, b. 1954.
Gelatin silver print. Purchase, The Horace W. Goldsmith Foundation Gift, 1992 1992.5147

OVERLEAF: **Subway Passengers, New York**, 1938. Walker Evans, American, 1903–1975.
Gelatin silver print. Gift of Arnold H. Crane, 1971 1971.646.20

Mannahatta

I was asking for something specific and perfect for my city,
Whereupon lo! upsprang the aboriginal name.

Now I see what there is in a name, a word, liquid, sane, unruly, musical,
  self-sufficient,
I see that the word of my city is that word from of old,
Because I see that word nested in nests of water-bays, superb,
Rich, hemm'd thick all around with sailships and steamships, an island
  sixteen miles long, solid-founded,
Numberless crowded streets, high growths of iron, slender, strong, light,
  splendidly uprising toward clear skies,
Tides swift and ample, well-loved by me, toward sundown,
The flowing sea-currents, the little islands, larger adjoining islands, the
  heights, the villas,
The countless masts, the white shore-steamers, the lighters, the ferry-boats,
  the black sea-steamers well-model'd,
The down-town streets, the jobbers' houses of business, the houses of
  business of the ship-merchants and money-brokers, the river-streets,
Immigrants arriving, fifteen or twenty thousand in a week,
The carts hauling goods, the manly race of drivers of horses, the
  brown-faced sailors,
The summer air, the bright sun shining, and the sailing clouds aloft,
The winter snows, the sleigh-bells, the broken ice in the river, passing along

up or down with the flood-tide
or ebb-tide,
The mechanics of the city, the
masters, well-form'd, beautiful-
faced, looking you straight in the
eyes,
Trottoirs throng'd, vehicles,
Broadway, the women, the shops
and shows,
A million people—manners free and
superb—open voices—
hospitality—the most
courageous and friendly young
men,
City of hurried and sparkling waters!
city of spires and masts!
City nested in bays! my city!

—Walt Whitman, American,
1819–1892

The Harbor of New York from the Brooklyn Bridge
Tower—Looking Southwest (detail), ca. 1877–94.
Nathaniel Currier, publisher, American, 1813–1888.
Hand-colored lithograph.
Bequest of Adele S. Colgate, 1962   63.550.132

Credits

Untitled, New York 1998. Mitch Epstein, American, b. 1952. Chromogenic print. Private collection